A BROKEN CHILDHOOD

A BROKEN CHILDHOOD

A True Story of Abuse

Lydia Ola Taiwo

Book Guild Publishing
Sussex, England

First published in Great Britain in 2011 by
The Book Guild Ltd
Pavilion View
19 New Road
Brighton, BN1 1UF

Typesetting in Garamond by
Nat-Type, Cheshire

Printed in Great Britain by
CPI Antony Rowe

A catalogue record for this book is available from
The British Library.

ISBN 978 1 84624 590 9

Contents

Acknowledgements

I would like to acknowledge my husband who has, for the past 20 years, stood by me and helped me to overcome the emotions and pain of the past. He sees the scars all over my body every day, but still provides the love and support I need on a daily basis.

I would like to thank our son Timothy, who took time to type up much of the script. I am sure he has learnt something from my past. Thanks also to my cousin Nicola for her continued inspiration and for reading over the script.

There are mothers, and there are mothers. There is the biological mother, and there are mothers who for one reason or another just come into your life to shape it for the years ahead. I am therefore glad to acknowledge my foster mum and dad, Mr and Mrs Coombes, for the love they showered on me when I was a baby and toddler.

Preface

In the summer of 1964, Mojisola (known as Ola) was born to a young couple at King's College Hospital in Camberwell, London. She was their first child. Soon after she was born, her parents placed her in what they referred to as 'foster' care – which was more like stand-in or proxy care. This particular practice was not uncommon among young married Nigerian students at the time. It was probably an affordable childcare option that kept children out of the way for weeks, months and occasionally years.

In some cases children remained with their foster families for a long while, with or without frequent visits from their own parents. Although the mainly white English working-class families were paid for their services, they effectively became surrogate parents to those children. This private arrangement was intended to help struggling students to focus on their jobs and studies. It probably saved Ola's life. In fact, her earliest memories of childhood date back to pleasant recollections of life with her foster family in the Sussex seaside town of Hastings.

When Ola was five years old, her parents took her back from her foster family to live with them in South London. Ola's early memories of her biological mother reveal a cruel and wicked woman. Some of the treatment Ola faced between the ages of five and twelve was terrible indeed. The very idea that 'loving' parents could inflict such abuse on their first child beggars belief, but the physical evidence of scars are consistent with Ola's account. She was abused verbally, physically and emotionally – and all this at the hands of her own mother and father. Even the courts and Social Services were well and truly deceived.

This book is not intended as a criticism of anyone or any organization. Neither is it an attempt to be vindictive. For Ola, writing this book is the first step towards coming to terms with seven years of torture which remain deeply etched in her memory. It is a personal, reflective account of a tough life. However, a decision to forgive her mother after 26 years finally released her from the pain and hurt. At the time of writing this book, many of the people mentioned are probably still alive. Although Ola cannot remember names of certain individuals, much effort has been put into protecting the identities of all, except those whose roles are significant in her life.

*   *   *

Ola's story is my story. This is my own account of what I experienced in those first impressionable twelve years of life.

Writing this book has been very challenging for me. It has made me revisit my past, and it has been both an emotional and a therapeutic experience. Please read this book with the assurance that a great deal of effort has been put into ensuring that the information is not exaggerated. I am certain that much of this information can be corroborated by research, bearing in mind that all events mentioned are over 30 years old at the time of writing. While events and memories may be subject to different interpretations, real evidence speaks for itself. Records, documents and data may be lost, mislaid, destroyed or deleted, but physical scars often remain visible for life.

This book is an account of my traumatic early life up to the age of twelve. Every single event in this book is true – the hospitals, the appearance of Social Services at my home at Lulworth House in Dorset Road, my teeth that were broken, my head injury and all the other appalling experiences. The evidence is there for everyone to see.

You might wonder if I had any good experiences with my parents. I do not know, because the abuse has overshadowed any good they may or may not have done. Although I still live with the scars and sometimes the pain and the memories still cause me to cry, I have forgiven my parents. It was hard and it still is, especially when I see the scars daily and I can only style my hair in a particular way as a result of the head injury.

It has taken twelve years to write this book, as small as it is, and that was because it took that long to come to the point of forgiving my parents. I did not realise that it was something I needed to do; I thought that all the pain, hurt and bitterness would automatically go away as I grew older. But they didn't; they became so deep seated within me that I felt even more hatred and revenge towards my parents rather than love. I was always sad and withdrawn, I felt my life was broken and I needed to be fixed.

It was not until I was counselled to write down all my experiences as a form of therapy, that I got some relief. It was so difficult to write because the more I wrote, the more tearful I became. While I was writing my story I heard about the death of Victoria Climbie on the BBC News. I was so sad that even within the twenty-first century child abuse is still on the increase, and still goes unnoticed. This motivated me not to just write as a therapy for myself, but to also make my book available globally for the world to know that child abuse is a serious issue that needs to be dealt with. Hopefully it will be remembered by all who read it, and will be a learning tool for social workers and parents/carers who have responsibility for children.

Does anyone really know what lies behind the mind of an abused child? It may be that it will never be known. An innocent child may have been murdered before their story is heard or, as a result of the trauma and lack of love, the child may have decided to join a gang, where they receive a false sense of 'love' that their parents did not give to them. Many of these children, if not counselled appropriately, will end up becoming more violent and may even go on to kill other innocent people.

What is love? What does love mean to an abused child? If you really want to know – love does not have any meaning. I thank God I am alive to tell my story because I know there is someone out there who needs to hear it.

1

Life in Foster Care

I learnt from an older relation that I was placed into foster care when I was about six months old. Nobody has ever explained why this happened to me, but I have found out that many Nigerians, especially in the 1960s, did this so they could earn a living while they studied. With the children out of the way, they could spend as many hours working as was necessary. It did not really matter what kind of job it was, as long as it paid the wages to cover their expenses.

I loved my foster parents, Mr and Mrs Coombes. They were kind and loving. They treated me as one of their own children. I did not realize that I was a little black girl living with a white family. Neither was I aware that I had different biological parents until I was five years old. My foster parents had a daughter and two sons of their own, and there were two other children in care besides myself. We all lived together in a very big house in St Leonards, Hastings.

Happy times

I sometimes went to play in the fields and the local park with my foster brothers and sisters. I remember that I enjoyed looking at horses and farm animals. I also loved feeding the ducks with breadcrumbs. I enjoyed living in the countryside, it was very peaceful and there were so many interesting things to do. What I loved most of all was walking in the fields with my foster brothers and sisters, picking strawberries and blackberries for baking a pie at home. Often, of course, we would end up eating most of them on the way home.

Then there was the annual summer fair, which was very exciting! I remember going on the roundabouts and the big wheel, as it was called then. I was as happy as could be. My foster mum always bought me loads of candyfloss and ice-cream on those occasions. Like most children, I loved all that. During the winter months, Mum would sit us all down after dinner with cups of Ovaltine and read us a bedtime story. We would gradually nod off to sleep. I was always carried to bed, and I loved that too. Although I cannot remember too many things from my time in Hastings, I knew I was loved and cared for. My foster mum treated us all equally and nicely, and if we did anything wrong we would all be told off in the same way.

I do remember two events quite vividly. The first was on a particular day when I followed my brother and sister to take a walk in the fields. We had to climb over a gate, but on the other side was a load of cow dung. It looked enormous and really monstrous to me. My big brother and sister climbed over the gate and expected me to do likewise. I froze and stood where I was. I panicked and started to cry and scream. I was afraid of the cow dung. My big brother beckoned to me to climb over the gate and jump over the cow dung. But you can imagine what I was thinking: if I did what they said, I would fall into the cow dung and be swallowed up! As he beckoned to me again and again, I cried louder and louder. Then I think my brother must have felt sorry for me, and he lifted me over the gate and clear of the cow dung. I held onto him tightly, grateful that he was there to protect me from the scary dung!

The second event I remember clearly was the day when my real parents came from London on a visit to Hastings to see me. I did not realise they were my real parents, or should I say my biological parents, until this very visit.

They told my foster parents that they wanted to take me home for a long weekend. My foster parents believed them and agreed. My foster mum packed a few clothes for the journey, along with my favourite teddy bear. My foster parents hugged and kissed me, telling me that they would see me the following Monday.

I was really scared, not quite knowing who these people were. I was not sure what to expect on this long weekend, but I assured myself that I would soon be back. After all, it was only for a weekend.

I was carried to the car by my foster mum, then she opened the car door and I got inside. My parents also got into the car. We were quickly on our way to London. I must have fallen asleep, because when I woke up I found myself in a strange house. I was being offered something to eat and drink.

Separation

My parents' home was 87 Flaxman Road in South London. The apartment was a single room with a large window. The room had been separated into two with a window blind. On one side of the blind there was my parents' bed and their belongings. I noticed a pile of plates, cups, spoons and food of all descriptions in a corner. On the other side of the blind were a couch, a small wooden chair, a radio-gram, as it was called then, and a black-and-white television.

I did not know that the couch was going to become my bed for a very long time indeed. My father got a bed sheet and blanket and made a place for me to sleep on the couch. I was given one of the pillows from my parents' bed and asked to change into my pyjamas and sleep. My parents did not say anything that night. The next day was Saturday. I was woken up, helped to brush my teeth, given a bath and provided with breakfast. Then I sat at home watching television. I do not remember much of what was said until Sunday, when I was informed by my real parents that I would not be returning to Hastings. My father said to me, 'The family in Hastings are just your foster parents, they were only meant to be looking after you for a period of time. We are your real parents and you will not be returning to them anymore, you will be going to school here in London.' Was I to be torn away from 'home' just like that? I could not believe it. I felt they had no regard for my feelings. Neither did they care what my foster parents would think about the lie they had told.

Gradually I realized that they were very serious. I started to cry. I cried and cried and cried. Tears streamed down my cheeks as I sobbed and sobbed. Who were these people who took me away from the ones who loved me so dearly? Why, why, why had I been treated in such a mean way?

I cried myself to sleep that night and had a dream which I can still remember to this day. In that dream I saw my foster mum standing with outstretched arms. I was so happy and ran towards her with all my energy. Gradually she began to disappear. I shouted, 'Mum, Mum, where are you? Wait for me!' But she had gone. I started to cry, and woke up still crying.

It was very traumatic for me. I had to learn to live with my real parents, whom I did not know and could not trust. I was not hugged or kissed; I was left alone to cry. I felt deceived. I was shocked by suddenly learning that I would be spending my life with these strangers who introduced themselves to me as my parents. I despised them for lying to me and my foster parents.

2

Rules, Punishment and Duties

It soon dawned on me that my life at Flaxman Road would be governed by certain rules and regulations. I had duties for which there were no rewards, but failure to perform them earned definite punishment. I was now in a home where learning time management was a priority. At just five years old, I needed to know that once the alarm clock went off I had to wake up and get out of bed. If I did not get out of bed, then I would be woken up with a severe beating with a whip. The whip was a length of the thick cable wire used for wiring houses in those days. If I did not eat my food in time I would get beaten too. If I got back from school late I would be severely punished.

My daily schedule was to get up from the couch on which I slept, fold up my bedding and place it in the corner of the room. I would brush my teeth and ease myself in the bathroom, get myself dressed for school and have breakfast, which was always cornflakes and hot milk. After this I would get my books ready for school, put on my coat and say goodbye to my mum – when she was around – on my way out of the door. I do not remember my mother or father ever walking me to school, although my heart yearned for this.

It seemed quite a distance for a young girl to walk alone from where we lived to the school. I would walk down Flaxman Road and turn right, then walk under the bridge and through Loughborough Estate until I reached the main road. Then I would cross the road and walk through the school gate of Loughborough Primary School into the playground.

I loved playing in the playground with my friends. I remember the clapping games, the ball and skipping games. I enjoyed going to school, I was never late. Life at school was great, simply because it was good to be far away from home. I did well at school and my class teacher and head teacher were quite impressed, because I was above average in all my subjects. I loved singing too. We used to do a lot of this during our assemblies. I remember one particular song, 'All things bright and beautiful, all creatures great and small, all things wise and wonderful, the Lord God made them all.' Who was God? I did not know at the time, but he surely kept me alive.

At lunchtime I would leave school to go home. Sometimes my mum would be at home and sometimes she would not. When she was not in, she would make arrangements so that I would be able to get the key for the door to get into the house. I had to get home in ten minutes to have my lunch. Lunch was only a packet of crisps and a drink of orange juice. My favourite flavour was cheese and onion or ready salted – not that I had a choice. I would sit on my couch where I normally slept and eat in silence, sipping at my orange juice. Once I had finished my 'meal' I would throw away my empty crisp packet and orange juice carton and get ready to walk back to school.

I walked the same route four times a day alone – come rain or sunshine. I would see passers-by on the way and sometimes some strange-looking people. I remember that once I was on my way home from school alone as usual, walking under the lonely bridge, when I saw a tramp. I was so scared that I ran all the way home. I could not tell anyone, not even my mum or dad.

Why could I not stay in school at lunchtime? Why was my life so different from everybody else's?

3

Hit By a Car

The accident happened when I was in the second year of primary school. My mum had beaten my hands with the wire cable the day before, because I came home late from school. She warned me that I must get home within 15 minutes of school closing, every day. I was so afraid of my parents that every day I would leave school as soon as the bell had gone, running all the way home. I dreaded going home, however, because there was always something that I had done wrong and would get a beating for. I was never rewarded for all the things I did right. It was like hell every day.

On this particular day I ran across the road as usual, but did not get across to the other side. I was hit by a car. I did not see it approaching. I cannot remember how far into the road I was when I was hit. All I do remember is my teacher dragging me back onto the pavement to lie me down on a coat. I started shouting, 'I've got to go home! I've got to get home or else I'll be in trouble!' I had cuts on both my legs and felt very hurt and dizzy. My teacher sent another teacher to call an ambulance and inform my parents. By this time she had lain me on my side, in

11

what I now know as the recovery position. She was talking to me, trying to keep me alert until the emergency services arrived.

The driver of the car that had hit me had sped off and witnesses could not obtain the car's registration number. Children were still being collected by their parents; other pedestrians were standing nearby looking at me, shocked and hoping that I would be OK. I could hear their concerned voices as parents scurried away with their young children – probably hiding the scene from their innocent gaze.

I could hear the ambulance siren in the distance. When it drew close to the school gate, the siren stopped. Within seconds one of the paramedics from the ambulance was speaking to me. He asked how I was feeling. The other man had the stretcher ready. I was just imagining what was in store for me from my mum. I did not know that many children my age did not survive such accidents on the streets of London. Mum had put so much fear in me that, in my mind, I just had to get home on time despite what had happened. I was not expecting care or concern, just the repercussions of getting home late. The ambulance driver got details of what had happened to me and was taking notes. When he had completed writing the report, he got into the ambulance and started the engine. I was on my way to King's College Hospital.

In the hospital

In the Accident and Emergency Department I waited to see the doctor and have my wounds dressed.

While my records were being checked I saw my father walking towards me. I was petrified. All kinds of questions were flooding my mind. What's going to happen to me now? Am I in trouble again? Will my mother believe me if I tell her I was hit by a car? Am I going to die? I looked at my dad and my gaze met his. He asked me how I was and enquired about what had happened. I explained that I had been trying to get home in time in order not to get into trouble. I made Dad aware of the time that Mum had said I needed to be home. There was no way that I could cover the distance between school and home in that time, without running as fast as my legs could carry me. Dad was not very happy. For a brief moment, I wondered whether he was heaping all the blame on me. My suspicion came close to being confirmed when he asked, 'Why didn't you check the road before crossing?' I explained to Dad that I had looked both right and left, but had not seen the car approaching.

One thing shocked me that day: my mother did not turn up at the hospital. I hated her for this. I just could not understand why she did not care. After all, she was the one who had warned me to come home on time, or else I would get another beating. That was what had scared me into running across the road in the first place.

While my dad and I were still talking, the nurse came over to attend to the bruises and cuts I had sustained on my knees and elbows. She cleaned the wounds using a colourless liquid and cotton wool, which stung painfully, and covered them with plasters. While she was doing this, she was speaking encouraging words to me. She was very tender and caring. I felt loved. After the nurse had completed the dressing she took me back to the doctor.

The doctor turned to me and asked how I was feeling. I said I felt a bit better. He checked my chest, my pulse and blood pressure. He also checked for any broken bones and then added the information to my case file. He felt satisfied that I was OK and had not broken any bones. He concluded that I could go home. He did say, however, that I should be more careful when crossing the road in future. I thanked the doctor for his advice. I knew that God must have spared my life for a reason. For that, I was grateful – and I still am. Dad and I then left the room and walked to the car. He drove us back in silence. I sat painfully in the back seat, considering what my next ordeal would be when I saw my mum.

Home without love

When we were just a stone's throw away from home, Dad started to talk to me, explaining the importance of crossing the road safely. I could not say whether he was speaking out of concern or just a sense of responsibility, but I listened attentively anyway. We got out of the car and headed up the stairs leading to the front of the house. Dad opened the front door with his key and asked me to walk in front of him. My bandaged and plastered limbs and bruised body must have been quite a sight to see as I cautiously made my entrance. I said hello to Mum as I walked in, she asked what had happened and I explained to her how I had been hit by a car. She said simply, 'You were just looking for attention!' That made me really, really sad. I knew that nothing could have been further away from the truth. I had almost got myself killed trying to impress my hard-to-please mum. 'Is this all she can say to me?' I thought. 'What if I had died?' There were no hugs, no sympathetic words or gesture of concern from my own mother. I loathed her even more because of that comment.

Mum had already prepared the evening meal, and she called our attention to it straight away. I ate my food in silence while Mum and Dad discussed things in Yoruba, a language I did not understand at the time. I felt ignored, even though I was not particularly expecting or seeking their attention. I was really hurt that I was just expected to 'chin-up' and get on with life even after a car accident. Despite the fact that my knees and elbows were very sore that night, I still had to make my own bed on the couch.

Lying down painfully on the couch, I went to sleep wondering if I would live for long. Would I survive to adulthood? What was I going to become? What did life hold for me in that house where there was no love? My parents did not know how I felt and I was too afraid to tell them. Still in pain, I fell asleep.

I woke up to another school day, plasters, bruises and all, and the same old routine. I went to school with the fear of facing the same road alone. I had no choice – I just had to get on with it. As I stepped out of the door I muttered a desperate prayer: 'Please God, if you are there, keep me safe and let me never be hit by a car again. I want to live long!'

4

Head Injury

There were two other families living at 87 Flaxman Road with us, in separate apartments. The landlord lived on the middle floor with his family, while another Nigerian couple lived in the basement with their daughter. The daughter was more or less the same age as I was. I do not know much about their personal circumstances, but I was aware that my parents were on talking terms with them.

A dilemma

On most school days when I got home, my parents were out. I used to sit at the foot of the stairs and wait for them to return. Sometimes – I believe out of compassion – when the couple saw me sitting on the stairs awaiting my parents' arrival, they would beckon to me to come into their home to stay with them until my parents arrived. Because I knew the family quite well I would accompany them into their home and play with their daughter until my parents arrived. They appeared to be happy to have me in their home during those times. This went on for some time, until one day I was told by my parents that I was not allowed in that family's home again, even if I was asked to come in. This, I later learnt, was the result of an argument that had broken out between them in my absence. I immediately had a problem. What should I say if they asked me in, on one of those lonely afternoons while I was waiting for my parents?

The next day, I did my best to adhere to my parents' instructions. But the family refused to see me sitting alone on the stairs, so they asked me in. I informed them that I was not allowed in their home. They insisted, stressing that they were not strangers to my parents, and neither was I a stranger in their home. Not wishing to appear rude, I went into the family's apartment downstairs, hoping that somehow my parents would understand my predicament. The family prepared some food, as they normally did around that time of the evening, and offered me something to eat. I do not quite remember what the meal was that evening, but I joined the family at the dining table, sitting next to my friend, their daughter. We spoke about school, friends and what we thought about our teachers.

After the meal, we sat in the living room to watch television. Within about 15 minutes there was a hard knock on the door. My heart started to pound. I was afraid, very afraid. I suddenly remembered that accepting the family's hospitality was a disobedience to my parents. My friend's mum opened the door and there stood my mum and dad. With my heart racing, I thought about what I was going to say. What would become of me? Would I survive the night? All these questions swiftly flooded my mind. When I saw the look on my parents' faces I knew that I was in a lot of trouble. I blurted out a muffled hello to both of them. They looked at me, but ignored my greeting. Both tersely thanked the family for having me.

A boot to the head

I walked briskly upstairs to our apartment, full of apprehension. The moment I got through the door I was ordered to 'stoop down'. I recall that this kind of corporal punishment requires you to bend down on one leg and, with the other leg lifted up, you place one hand on your back, using one finger of the other hand to touch the floor for balance. I had to stay balanced for at least 30 minutes – a painful and difficult posture even for an adult. I was only a child. While I was in this position, I was being queried about my visit to the family downstairs. Before I could answer, I had received a kick to the back of my head from my dad's black boots. Not just once – I received two or three kicks to the back of my head. I did not see them coming. By the time I had received the second kick, blood was dripping from my head and I had fallen to the floor. They must have been hard-toe boots. I was in deep pain. I could not answer the questions my dad continued to ask.

My head was throbbing painfully when, for the first time ever in my life, I heard my mother shout to my father to stop. He stopped and left me there on the floor, still bleeding. My mum pulled me up and quickly got a wad of tissue to wipe away the blood.

In an attempt to stop the bleeding, she held the tissue to my head until blood was no longer dripping. My father, who was a trained nurse before his arrival in the UK, should have checked the wound he had inflicted on me, at the very least to confirm that the bleeding had stopped. I do not think my parents actually understood the extent of the injury I sustained that evening.

I was told to go to bed, so I changed from my school uniform into my pyjamas. I then got my bedding from the corner, laid it on the couch, got into my bed and closed my eyes.

I was in an agonizing pain. My head was throbbing and aching so badly that I had to hold my head to go to sleep. I do not know how long it took me to fall asleep that night. All I can remember was that I woke up in the middle of the night crying and screaming, because I was in so much pain. My father, still lying in bed, asked what the matter was. I replied to him, crying out in pain, that my head was hurting.

When the light was switched on, I could see that my pillow was covered in blood. Quickly my father got out of bed and when he saw the blood he shouted, 'Eweje!' ('Look at blood!') I had been bleeding continuously from my head while I was asleep.

My parents had a frantic discussion between themselves. Some of the things they said I neither heard nor understood. I continued to hold my aching, throbbing head. However, I heard them agree that they had to call the ambulance service immediately. Some of the blood had clotted and locks of my hair were stuck together. The injury was still bleeding profusely down my neck. Dad called the ambulance service and told them that I had a head injury, sustained from a fall down the stairs. What were the odds of that happening? This was a single-room apartment, where the only flight of stairs was situated outside the room.

Waiting for the ambulance seemed to take a long time as the pain grew worse. Meanwhile, I could hear my parents telling me the likely questions I would be asked and the responses I should give. I was being coached to tell blatant lies. In my pain, I knew I had no choice in the matter. I feared for what could be in store for me if I did not toe the line. Firstly, I should tell them that I slipped and fell down the stairs. Secondly, I should say there was no one around to see what happened. My parents were teaching me to lie to get them out of trouble.

Hospital again

The ambulance service arrived, the paramedics came upstairs. One asked my parents what had happened, while another was attending to me, applying wads of cotton wool to the injury to stop the bleeding. The paramedics then carried me into the ambulance where they made sure that I was comfortable. The driver quickly sped off, blue lights flashing on the way to King's College Hospital once again.

Within minutes we had arrived and my stretcher was whisked from the ambulance straight to the Accident and Emergency Department. I was immediately attended to because I was still bleeding profusely, and an ice pack was applied to the back of my head to stop the bleeding. I was in so much pain, I felt as if my head was going to blow up.

When the doctor asked me how I sustained the injury, I responded as coached by my parents that I fell down the stairs. I could see by the puzzled look on his face that he found that difficult to believe or inconsistent with the injury. He hummed and asked how that happened. I said that I slipped and fell down the stairs. He must have suspected that my story was not a true account and promptly probed further. 'What did you slip on?' I could not answer that question. I just stared at him because I did not know what to say. That question was not covered in my coaching. I was lying because I was afraid of what my parents would do to me if I told the doctor the truth.

The doctor requested that I went for an X-ray to make sure that I had not broken my skull and to check for any internal bleeding. As I was rushed to the X-ray department by the nurses, my parents followed along. Mum and Dad were very anxious to know what the doctor had asked and what my responses were. They asked me as I was being taken to the X-ray department. Their calm but concerned expressions masked the anxiety I could sense in their questions. I told my parents that the doctor asked what happened and that I told him I fell down the stairs.

The X-ray investigation took about 20–30 minutes in a private cubicle. My head was aching and still bleeding profusely. I was taken to one of the X-ray cubicles where I was gently laid down on a table, my head being supported by a nurse with an ice pack on the injury. I was screaming and yelling from the pain – it felt as if my head was going to burst open. I could hear someone asking me to stay still as the X-ray was being taken. The machine made a slight whirring noise. I heard that the radiographer needed to take further X-rays at different exposures, and I continued to scream with pain. Finally the X-rays were all completed. I had to wait on the stretcher in the waiting room with my parents while the results came through. It was an agonizing wait. I hated my father for what he had done to me. I cried for two reasons: for the pain of my injury, and also for the torture I had received from the man who was meant to be my dad.

Just before the results came through, a nurse came along and gave me some painkillers. She also took me away to another cubicle to receive treatment to my head. She cleaned the wound, applied a dressing and covered it in a bandage. The bandage was wrapped around the top of my head, so that my hair was entirely covered. I was then taken back to the doctor with my X-ray results. The doctor looked through the report and was happy to see that I did not have a skull fracture or haemorrhage to the brain. He did, however, inform my parents that I needed to be off school for two to three weeks while the injury healed. The doctor discharged me and gave my parents a prescription for further painkillers. By this time it was early in the morning. With the painkillers taken, I must have been so exhausted that I fell asleep. I do not remember how I got home. I woke up to find myself on my parents' bed. I was treated as an invalid for that day only.

So alone

For the next two weeks I stayed at home unable to go to school. I was home alone with my head aching really badly. My parents did not stay at home with me during those two weeks – they went to work. I was so sad that neither of my parents cared enough to stay at home and watch over me. I was under eight years old. They did not even *seem* to care. I was left with food to eat for breakfast and lunch. I woke up each day with pain; I had to use my two hands literally to lift my head from the pillow to get up out of bed. Every morning during those two weeks I would get up, brush my teeth and have some cornflakes to eat. Then I took my painkillers and returned to bed, using my hands to support my head as I lay down again. In the evening, when my parents arrived back from work, I would have dinner with them, take the last dose of my medication for the day and then make my bed on the couch where I would sleep until morning.

As the two weeks went on, I felt better and the pain and throbbing headaches subsided. My head did heal, but for many years no hair grew around the site of the injury. The scar area remains bald to this day.

There was really no communication between myself and my parents. I thought I was an inconvenience. Maybe I was. I was never kissed, hugged or embraced by either of my parents. I felt unloved. I was just existing, living in a strange, inhospitable environment. I really wanted someone to love me, to care for me, to talk to and with me, but there was no one. Still, that was my dream, my hope and prayer in those days.

The head injury healed with time, but it left me with physical, psychological and emotional scars.

5

Money Trouble

In 1971 the UK changed over to decimal currency, pounds and pence. The old currency consisted of pounds, shillings and pence, and that was what I had only just learned in school:

12d (pence) = 1s (shilling)
20s = £1

The new decimal system was different:

100p = £1.00
100p = 240d
1p = 2.4d

Sometimes you went to the shops, spent old pounds, shillings and pence and got your change in new pound notes and pennies. This was very confusing. I was only seven years old. Like many of my peers at the time, my young brain could not manage the currency conversion outside the classroom.

My mother, however, expected me to be a super-girl, a genius mathematician able to count in decimal pence and pounds immediately! Whenever I was sent to the shops, I had to work out the change I received using the new system. I was more confused than ever. Whenever I got my change from the shopkeeper, I counted it wrong all the time, despite always getting severely beaten with my mum's instrument of choice – a thick length of electrical cable, with the copper wire visible inside it. I was beaten all over my body. I always had marks to show for the beatings I had received. Even to this day, the scars are still visible on my back, calves, legs, head and arms. It was terrible.

Beaten

On one fateful day I was sent to the shop to buy some bread and milk. I left the house and walked down the road to Mr Bailey's shop at the junction. This time I hoped that Mum would not question me about the change. I trusted Mr Bailey to give me the right change. He was a very nice man. I knew him to be a person of integrity: if you gave him more money than was required, he would make you aware and then return the excess back to you. I said good morning to Mr Bailey as I entered the shop, went over to the passageway where the milk and bread were kept, picked one of each of the items and went to the counter to pay. I handed Mr Bailey the money I was given by my mum, and he passed me back the change. I thanked him, knowing that he would have given me the right change, but I could not get my head around how much it was. I walked slowly home, deeply scared of what my next ordeal would be.

I was learning about money at school, of course, but this was difficult. It was so hard for me to count correctly under pressure. I needed a crash course or a special programme on the new currency to placate my mother. When I finally got home, my mother asked me how much change I had. I was speechless and started to move backwards. When I could go no further, I stopped. Mum got the cable and gave me a thrashing. It seemed to last more than an hour. Cuts appeared all down my legs and arms. I was bleeding. All the while, however, I was trying as best as I knew how to count those coins. Finally I managed to get the sums right, and only then did Mum decide to leave me alone. I was in so much pain and could not understand why she had done that to me. I still have not forgotten to this day. Little was I to know that the worst was yet to come over the next few years.

For the next two weeks I had to wear thick blue tights to cover the marks on my legs, to hide the cuts from my dad and from the school authorities. I felt very uncomfortable wearing the tights because this all happened in the hot summer months. I was in so much pain, not just from the cuts and bruises, but in my heart. These were the questions that were always in my mind: 'Will I survive this? Why am I here? Why do I have to go through this pain? Why was I taken away from my foster parents who loved and cared for me?' I could find no answers.

During the next few days my dad observed that I was wearing thick tights every day and was curious to find out why. He called me over and asked, 'Why are you wearing thick winter tights during summer? Aren't you hot?' I could not say anything. He then asked me to take the tights off. He was amazed to see my legs with so many scars and bruises. He asked me why my legs were so badly scarred. I told him about the money I had been unable to count correctly when Mum sent me to the shop a couple of days earlier. He was angry with Mum and had a very heated argument with her that evening. Dad told Mum that she had no right to do what she did to me. He said, 'She's only seven years old. How do you expect her to know the difference? Even the adults are finding it confusing.' Mum got angry and left the room. I was now even more afraid, knowing full well that Mum would take out her anger on me whenever my father was not at home.

Things did not get any better. I was a stranger in my own home. There was no communication, no smiling, no playtime, nothing. I became very quiet and never talked. I was only happy when I was left alone at home. Those were the times when I was not afraid, simply because there was nothing I could do wrong or be blamed for.

6

Abuse and Trauma

I remember that a few months after the incident with the change I was taken to Brighton for the birthday party of one of my cousins. My parents informed me that I had a first cousin living in Brighton. I was older than her by two years. She was living in Brighton with her foster parents. Her real mother was my mother's older sister, whom I did not really know at the time. The birthday party turned out to be one of my happy memories. It was lovely to be at a party for a change! I saw many happy faces, both children and adults. The menu consisted of chicken, sausage rolls, popcorn, cakes of all sizes, sweets, fruit salad, jelly, lots of drinks and ice-cream.

We played many games. I took part in pass-the-parcel, musical chairs and hide-and-seek. There was a dancing competition in which I did not get involved, because I did not know how to dance. I stayed in one corner and filled myself with sweets and popcorn. The party lasted for about two hours. That was the day I met my cousin for the first time. I spoke to her only a little, however, as she was a stranger! We did get to know each other much more over the years that followed, and we have become as close as sisters today. As we said goodbye to each other, her foster mother gave us goodie bags. My bag contained a piece of cake, a lollipop and many colourful sweets.

We got back to London quite late that night. We had to take a coach, which took a very long time. There was silence all the way home. When we got into the apartment I was asked to go straight to bed. I made my bed on the couch as usual and attempted to sleep. I found it difficult. I had a bad tummy ache! I tossed and turned, and although I was feeling very sick, I did manage to fall asleep eventually. Later that night I vomited all over my bedding and the floor. I did not know what to do, neither did I realize how messy it was. I was too scared to tell my sleeping mum that I felt ill. At the time, I was so weak that I fell asleep again.

When my mother woke up she was furious. She started shouting at me, 'Get up and clean this up!' I got out of bed, still feeling unwell. I had to take off all the bedding from the couch without help and use the sheets to wipe off excess vomit from the couch and the floor. I had to wash the bedding myself – and I did not do a good job. Mum slapped me on my face out of anger because I had ruined the bedding and it all had to be thrown away. How could I, at eight and a half years old, wash such large bed sheets? At the very least, I needed care, not violence.

On another occasion my mother had prepared a Yoruba (south-western Nigerian) meal. Can you imagine being raised on an English diet, having spent the first five years of your life in an English home, and then being forced to adapt instantly to eating

African food? What a change, a sudden and difficult change! On this particular day we were eating *amala* – black pudding, as we used to call it – and spicy spinach. I was eating with my parents from the same plate, using my fingers. I had not been taught the technique of eating such food. Of course I was making a mess of it, with finger marks left all over my side of the plate. From my mum's point of view, it looked repugnant. She became very agitated. I just did not know how to partition the food with my fingers. Then I got some of the spinach stuck in my throat and began to choke. I vomited onto the meal and the table.

My mum was furious and ordered, 'Start eating the food!'

'Like that?' I thought. 'With the vomit?'

My dad said in disgust, 'Leave it.'

My mother looked at me and repeated the warning again: 'Eat the food like that! I will not be making another meal.'

I got scared, knowing what my mother could do. So I started to use my fingers to gather the food mixed with vomit and was about to put it into my mouth when my dad shouted, 'Stop!'

With that my dad, who by that time was also enraged, got up and ordered my mother to take away the food and clear the table. She refused to do either and began to argue with him. The next thing I knew was that my father took the cable that Mum used to use on me, and started to hit her with it. My mother began to scream and cry. I started to cry too, terrified and unable to understand what in the world I could do to please my parents. My presence in this house seemed to be the cause of so much trouble. I could not help thinking that they should have left me where I was in Hastings.

Finger and thumb cut

My father used to use Wilkinson blades to shave in those days. Mum would also use the blades to cut her nails. One day when my parents were not at home I decided to cut my long nails using the double-sided blade I sometimes saw them use to cut their nails. I went to the table where the blades were kept, took one of the blades and started to cut my fingernails. In the process I gave myself big cuts on my finger and thumb.

The cuts bled badly and I went to the toilet to collect tissue paper to stop the bleeding. I did not tell my parents about the cuts as I was so afraid of the trouble I would get into. I cannot remember how my mother found out. She told me off and said she would have to treat the cuts. She went to the kitchen, filled the kettle with water and placed it on the cooker. In those days there were not many electric kettles around. We had one of those metal kettles that whistle when the water boils. When she heard the kettle whistle my mum went to get it, placed an old cloth on the table and put the kettle on top of it. She then said, 'Now, I will treat your finger and thumb.'

I had a feeling this was going to be painful. She told me to place my thumb and finger on the kettle. I started to cry, telling her it was hot and would burn me. She grabbed my hand and placed my finger and thumb on the kettle, pressing them down. I started to scream and yell. No one came to my aid. It seemed to last for several minutes. During this time I shouted at her, 'I hate you!' and she shouted back, 'I hate you too!'

My thumb felt very sore and swollen, and it was blistered. My heart was hurt and full of hatred towards her, but there was nothing I could do to escape from her. My dad was out when this happened, but I could not tell him when he came back home that evening. I had become so withdrawn that I rarely had a conversation with anyone outside school – including my parents.

I thought she wanted me dead

It was during the cold winter of 1972 when I lost the buttons on my coat and could not find them. This was not intentional; I did not know that the buttons were loose and they just dropped off – where and when that happened I did not know.

Of course my mum wanted to know what had happened to the buttons and why they were missing from my coat. I could not give her a satisfactory answer. She thought I was lying and said I should tell her the truth. Then she held my nose and mouth. I could not remember when the buttons went missing or how they got lost. She held my nose so tightly that I could not breathe, and I struggled with her. She let me go for a while and laughed, then she started the treatment again. To save my life, I told her that I remembered and made up a story that the buttons fell off while I was on my way to school. I was afraid of dying and I was certain I was being suffocated. Finally she left me alone.

Again my mind teemed with questions: 'How did I survive that? Why is my life so different? Why can't I experience love or care from my own mother? Why won't my parents show me love? Does she want me dead? Was I a mistake? Was I an unwanted child?' I wanted to be like other children I saw, talking and playing with their parents in the park or just walking down the road, hand in hand. Would I ever experience this?

New baby

All the while I thought I was an only child. Soon, however, I noticed that my mother was pregnant. In fact, this was my mother's third pregnancy: it was not until that time that I found out I had a three-year-old sister in foster care.

My brother was born on 26 December 1972. I do not know which hospital he was born in. I remember that I stayed home alone when Dad took Mum into hospital that evening. For dinner I ate some biscuits that were on the table, as there was no food prepared for me to eat and I did not know how to cook. Mum and Dad came home the following day with my baby brother. I had to be actively involved in emptying nappy contents and soaking the nappies in boiling water (disposable nappies were not very available back then). I had to learn how to carry the baby and care for him when my mother needed to take a rest.

For religious purposes, my brother had to be circumcised by a rabbi, and this was done in the same room where I was present. I did not understand what was happening. My brother screamed all through the operation. I felt so sorry for him, but did not know what to do, I was so distraught. What were they doing to him? He was only a baby! My own experiences had filled me with fear for his life and continued existence in the family. He continued screaming in between sleeps for the next 24 hours. He could hardly sleep, and neither could I. When he cried, my mum would offer him milk to drink all through his ordeal.

One weekend morning a few months later, after my breakfast, my mum told me that she wanted to go for a walk and I had to look after my brother while she was out. He was asleep on the bed. My mum had been out for about 15 minutes when my brother rolled off the bed. I caught him just in time, but he started to cry. I held him close to me and patted him gently on the back so he would stop crying. While he was still crying, however, my mum returned and demanded to know what I had done to my brother. I told her I had not done anything, but she did not believe me. If my brother had suffered a serious injury that day, I would not have been able to live with the guilt. Today, leaving such a young girl in sole charge of a baby would be treated as gross neglect and irresponsibility.

It was clear to me that Mum seemed different in her behaviour to my brother. She cared so much for him: why could she not express some love to me too? Maybe she preferred boys. If so, whose fault was it that I came as a girl? I am happy to be a girl, very happy indeed. Maybe, I wondered, she was not loved as a child herself.

Life went on with nothing exciting happening. My parents gave me a lot of beatings to 'train me up'. I cannot remember once having time to play with my little brother or friends. There were simply too many chores and too much homework to fill my day.

7

Life at Dorset Road

The following year we moved from 87 Flaxman Road to a council flat in south-west London – Flat 47, Lulworth House in Dorset Road, SW8. The flat consisted of three bedrooms, a large hallway, a living room, a separate toilet and bathroom and a kitchen. I recall that my sister arrived from Hastings to join the family at Lulworth House. I do not remember how and when exactly, but I think she was about five years old. We became a family of five. My sister and I gradually got acquainted with each other. We did not have a choice. We just had to get on with existing as sisters. Mum had arranged how we were going to live in the house.

My parents had their own room. I was also given my own room, while my brother and sister shared a room. Dorset Road was quite a distance from Flaxman Road. For that reason my parents changed my school to one more local. The name of my new school was Wyvil Primary School, on Wyvil Road SW8. I was nine years old when I started at Wyvil. I spent two years there. I still had to walk to and from school alone.

My daily duties at home increased. I was

responsible for vacuum-cleaning the whole three-bedroom flat and washing the toilet and bathroom. I had to babysit my siblings when my parents were not at home, and plait my hair and my sister's hair every week. I had to make sure there were no pots or plates in the sink overnight, wash my school uniforms and make sure all my homework from school was completed on time. How on earth could a nine-year-old carry out all these chores success-fully? But somehow I did. If I failed to complete my chores daily or weekly, I would get up to twelve lashes in one go. The punishment went like this: I would take off all my clothes under warning and lie on the carpet in the living room, and my mother would start to hit me with the thick wire. If for any reason I put my hand in the way or moved, she would start the counting from one to twelve again. It does not seem right, does it? Yet it happened, and today I have all the marks to show for it.

My mother had to find a local childminder to look after my brother, because she needed to go back to work. I was the one responsible for taking him to the childminder before I went to school and for picking him up on my way back from school. He was so heavy when he was a baby, but I had to carry him and climb up two flights of stairs to get to the childminder's flat behind Lulworth House. Another responsibility was to take care of my sister and brother when we all got back from school. My sister could not get a space in my school and had to go to St Stephen's CE School just down Dorset Road. It was quite easy for her to get back home.

Buying friendship

I was a child who needed acceptance. I needed someone to love me. My parents did not show affection to me, and I looked for it at school among my peers. In the hope of earning friendship, I brought some of my things from home to school and gave them away to my friends. My father had bought me a Parker pen which I decided to give away to a classmate of mine, so that I would become her best friend. Unfortunately, I did not know that my parents were going to ask me for the pen that day.

By now I had learnt from them that lying does get people out of trouble. What a warped moral foundation! When my parents enquired about the pen, I told them that I did not know where it was and that I did not take it. I was afraid to tell them the truth. My mother did not believe me and she told me that she would continue to beat me until I told her the truth. She took the wire cable and began to hit me all over my body. I cried and began to tell her what had happened to the pen. 'I gave it to my friend!' I shouted. She then hit me even more because I had lied. I was hurting all over. There were cuts and bruises all over my body, my legs and my arms.

The following day at school, the playground supervisor spotted me and saw the cuts and bruises on my arms and legs. She asked me what had happened. I explained to her that I gave a pen to my friend and lied about it at home, and because I lied I was beaten by my mother. The supervisor was taking notes as I spoke to her; she asked a few more questions that day. I did not realize that she was taking notes of all my answers. She put her arm round me and said I would be OK, I should not worry.

That evening we were visited by two social workers, who asked questions regarding the incident I had reported in school. One asked me whether I had been beaten, but I lied and said no when I saw my mum's stern look. I noticed the social workers took some notes, and then they left.

All hell broke loose once that door was shut. My mum beat me so hard, I thought she was going to kill me. She told me that if I ever told anyone else about the beatings, I would be in even more trouble.

The social services did not call again to the best of my knowledge. Neither did my school follow up the incident. That was the end of the matter for them, I guess. It did not end the abuse for me.

Forced to learn and adapt

I was beginning to learn the different house chores and get used to my new responsibilities, when my mother decided that now was the best time for her elder daughter to learn how to cook. So I started cooking lessons. I thought the intention was that once I got home with my siblings, I could quickly cook something for all of us to eat if we were hungry. I did not know that my parents had a family friend whose child was two years older than me, who could cook very well. It only gradually dawned on me that my parents really wanted to raise me to outshine that child in the kitchen – and probably in other areas also. They relished moments when they could pose and brag about my accomplishments to their friends. How was I to cope? Life felt so unfair.

I had to learn how to make Nigerian dishes. *Eba* was a typical example. *Eba* is made from *gaari* (extracted cassava dough which has been oven-dried). This can be eaten with any one of a variety of soups (such as spinach, *egusi*, *okro*, etc.). *Eba* is prepared by adding the *gaari* to boiling water off the cooker. You then allow the *gaari* to soak up the water and cook, before stirring it into a smooth dough. When correctly prepared it is meant to have no lumps. My *eba* always had lumps and was not always cooked properly. I had to eat it like that; my mother would cook another lot for my siblings. She used to say to me, 'If you eat it like that this time, you will know how to make sure it is cooked the next time you have to prepare it.' That summarized my cooking lessons. I detested her for this. Although rice was the easiest meal to cook, still I would sometimes get it burnt and would have to eat it burnt too.

One day Mum cooked us *amala* (black pudding) and *okro* soup. The food was still hot and I did not like it. Mum stood close by with the cable wire in her hand. She shouted, 'Hurry up and eat!' I turned towards her to tell her that I was eating but it was too hot. The next thing I knew, blood was dripping from my head. She had hit my head with the wire. That was how I got another serious cut on my forehead. The scar is still visible to this day. I did not say a word. I just cried and cried, stuffing myself with the food I hated.

My parents were always having parties with other Nigerian friends. Most times I was the chef. I had to learn how to cut fresh chicken into small pieces using a sharp knife. I had a lot of finger cuts as a result. On one occasion I cut the gall bladder by mistake, making the chicken taste very bitter. I never really knew the power of the bile in the gall bladder until then. I had a crash lesson on chicken anatomy from Dad that afternoon. Surprisingly, I was not beaten, but the chicken was not edible.

Mum used to give me hot chocolate, which she expected me to drink up while it was still boiling hot. I burnt my tongue and mouth so many times doing that. I have a few brown taste buds on my tongue today which I attribute to the effect of those hot drinks. She would stand behind me and expect me to swallow the hot chocolate drink, just like that. Most times I drank it under duress with the liquid burning my mouth. I was usually compelled to stand up with my back to her, so she could hit me from behind with a stick if I was too slow.

On one occasion it was my head that the broomstick landed on. My head made a sizzling sound and started to pour with blood. I started to cry. When the blood became too much, my mum pulled me into the bathroom and put my head under the bath tap. The water from the hot tap was scalding, the bath was full of blood, I was screaming, but no one came to my aid. When she was satisfied, my mum then poured methylated spirit on the wound and covered it with some cotton wool. She sent me to bed immediately after that. I could hardly feel the sting of the methylated spirit as the wound was aching so badly from the blow and the scalding water. Did I deserve this? I thought sometimes it would have been better if I had not been born. I believed no one deserved such callous, heavy-handed treatment, no matter what they had done.

The injury was not treated in hospital. I was treated at home by my mum, who cleaned it daily with cotton wool and methylated spirit. It really did sting and hurt. I could not tell anyone at school, especially after the last beating I had sustained when the social services came to our home. The head injury did heal. It left the biggest scar on my head, however, and is another place that remains bald to this day.

Due to the abuse and trauma I experienced over not eating my food in time, I hated eating. I used to dislike mealtimes intensely. When my mother was not looking or was not in the same room, I would pack lumps of the hated food into my shoes. I would then throw the shoes under my bed, where a lot of fungi started growing. You can imagine what my room smelt like after a few weeks! However, I did not realize anything would happen. I expected the smell to go away soon, but of course it got worse. My parents began to notice some bad odours coming from my room. They asked my sister and I to search my room and bring whatever it was that smelt out of it. After we got the stinking contents out from under the bed, I got beaten with wire again for hiding food in my shoes.

I still disliked the 'foreign' foods. When I saw that my first strategy was not working, I had to think of another idea very quickly. 'If I put the food in the toilet and flush it, surely it will disappear?' I thought.

I tried it once, hiding bits of *amala* and *eba* in my clothes and telling my mum that I needed to go to the toilet. I emptied the food into the toilet and flushed it away.

Once I realized that the food could go down the loo, I repeated the trick as often as I could. I would then tell my mum that I had finished my food. My parents never found out, but this is what became of the food that I did not like and would not eat. I loved chips, egg, spaghetti and sausages and ate those with great speed. However, we did not eat such food often.

I did not know that at such a young age not eating enough could lead to some form of illness. I started to complain of stomach ache in school and my parents were informed about it. My father took me to the doctor. This was Dr Burns's surgery: I cannot remember the exact location, but it was within the borough of Lambeth. The doctor told my father that I needed to eat properly, as I was coming down with a stomach ulcer. He gave me some prescribed medication to use for a week and warned that I needed to start eating well from then on. I realized that somehow I had to start eating the Nigerian food.

8

Progress at School

I loved school, and I enjoyed learning. I enjoyed my English, maths, drama and literature lessons. I did not like PE, however, because we had to wear shorts and a short-sleeved top. This exposed most of my body, showing all the scars of previous beatings. My peers at school often asked me questions about the cuts and bruises that they saw. I always had to lie to them, telling them that I fell or that I cut myself.

My school report was always good. All my teachers were pleased with my progress. When I was in Year 6, my head teacher, Mr Hartley, requested a meeting with my parents. A letter was written to them giving them an appointment time and date. My parents asked me the night before what I had done wrong at school. I told them, 'Nothing.' They did not believe me, but I knew within my heart that I had done nothing wrong.

The following day my parents went along with me to school to see the head teacher. Mr Hartley commended them for my progress in my studies. He told them that I was doing so well that it would be good if I could attempt the Common Entrance 11-Plus exams for a grammar school place for the 1975 academic year. My parents were keen to take the advice. My father got the forms to register me for the exams. I was then provided with practice test papers to assist me in preparation.

Finally, the day of the examination came. I was not nervous. I loved studying and I found the tests quite interesting. I was given a mathematics paper and an English paper to do. The mathematics paper was a bit difficult, but the English paper I found much easier. We were told in the hall that day that the results would be out within three months.

When the results arrived, it was my father who broke the good news that I had passed. I was very pleased. Dad said that I needed to attend an interview to enable the school to finalize their selection of students for the 1975/76 session.

An opportunity lost

In those days, both potential students and their parents were interviewed. My parents and I went for the interview in West Norwood where the school was located. When we arrived at the school gate we followed the posted directions to get to the venue for the interviews. There were a lot of other children seated with their parents, also waiting for their interviews. My parents and I sat down alongside them and waited our turn.

When my name was called I went into a room where I saw three women sitting behind a long table. Nervously, I greeted them. 'Good morning,' they responded and asked me to take my seat.

I was asked a series of questions. The one I remember most clearly was this: 'If you had £25,000, what would you do with it?' I answered that I would spend most of it and save the rest.

After my interview, I was asked to call my parents in. I sat down on a chair outside the room to wait for them. I do not know what happened behind those doors, but suddenly I heard my father's raised voice, shouting angrily at whoever it was who was interviewing them. I concluded that it was all over for me: I did not see how I could be considered for admission now. An opportunity lost!

And truly it was. I received a letter that week that only confirmed my deepest fears. I was very sad that I was not given admission to that grammar school. I resigned myself to life in a state secondary school. Having worked so hard to pass the grammar school entrance examination, it was not the outcome I expected. It was disappointing, to say the least.

I was finally given admission to Vauxhall Manor Secondary School, a local authority school. My father took me to the school to have a look round and also to pick up the school brochure. I was afraid, apprehensive, scared, anxious and alone, thinking about this school, a big new school. How was I going to cope? Would I survive? Would I meet the targets set for me? Would I have good friends? Would I have any friends at all? What would happen to me? I kept asking all these questions in my heart, but got no answers.

9

Summer Holidays and New School

I did not really enjoy the summer holidays, as most of the time I was home alone with my sister and brother. My parents used to leave us at home most of the day anyway, but it felt even longer when it went on for almost six weeks. This particular summer, I was alone at home; I think my siblings went to the childminder. One night my mother warned me that there had been a lot of killings of young children, especially black children, when they opened the door to strangers. This scared me seriously. She said that if I wanted to stay alive, I should not open the door if someone knocked. My heart started to race ahead of me, I was so afraid. I was more than afraid. Given that we had never had a visit when my parents were out up till then, I had no reason to expect anyone. I did not have any friends who could come round to my house to play.

Secret funfair

While my parents were out at work the next day, there was a knock at the door. I did not answer, but then I heard a voice I recognized. It was my uncle, father to my cousin who lived in Brighton. I opened the door for him and saw my cousin also standing by his side. My uncle told me he had come to pick me up to take me out to Battersea Funfair with my cousin. I was so excited! I got dressed, put on my shoes and socks and followed my cousin and uncle downstairs to the car. He drove in silence all the way to Battersea Park, while my cousin and I sat in the back of the car and talked about all our experiences. I told her about all the things I had suffered at the hands of my mother, showing her the scars too.

When we arrived at Battersea Funfair there were various rides to go on. We had candyfloss and hot-dogs to eat. I really had a good time, especially on the big wheel and the merry-go-round. After we had been at the funfair for about three hours we started to head back home. I got home before my parents arrived. Thank God for that! I never did tell them that I had been out with my cousin and uncle.

A ruined visit

By the time I was ten years old, my housework was occasionally extended to cleaning the bathrooms and toilets during weekends. On one such day, my twin cousins came round on a visit and passed the night at our home. This was a rare opportunity for me to meet with and relate to other relatives. My cousins and I woke up early that morning and got ourselves ready for the day. After I had carried out my normal duties, Mum instructed me to clean the bathroom and toilet. This included the floors, the doors and the windows.

The tasks were so many and would take a lot of time to complete. I got started immediately. Fortunately, my cousins offered to help. I gladly shared out the work between us. I appreciated their offer of help – but it only led to trouble and painful consequences. The blame was not theirs, however. I got bowls of warm soapy water and soft sponges for the three of us to use to clean the windows, doors, sink and bath. While we were cleaning, a lot of the water splashed onto the floor. We quickly got the mop and tried to clear it up so that we would not slip or fall on the floor. As we were getting on with this, Mum came through the door and looked around. I could see the anger on her face.

She started shouting, complaining that I had made the floor wet. She came up to me and slapped my face, narrowly missing my eye. I could feel warm blood trickling down the right side of my face. Did I deserve this? I was cleaning the house as I had been asked. My cousins were petrified. They ran into the sitting room as quickly as they could, leaving us in the bathroom. I started to mop up the water that had been spilt, crying silently at the same time. After about 30 minutes my dad arrived home. I said hello to him. He looked at me and asked what had happened to my head. I explained what had happened – that I had accidentally poured water on the floor while my cousins and I tried to clean the windows and the doors. Dad was furious and could not hide his anger – he went to see Mum in the bedroom, where an angry exchange of words broke out between them.

Dad told my cousins and I to go out on the balcony in front of the house and play. Within minutes my mother called me into the sitting room and asked me to remove the clothes I was wearing. She said she had bought them. She told me to go and get the clothes my father had bought me and wear those instead. How was I to know which clothes were bought by my dad and which were bought by my mum?

Dad said to me, 'Don't take those clothes off. I bought them, so wear them.'

Mum shouted, 'Take them off!'

Dad said, 'No!'

I was afraid for my life.

I was more afraid of my mum than my dad, however, and I began to take off the dress I was wearing. It was over my neck by this time. My mother came up to me and almost strangled me with the cloth round my neck. I did not say a word. I just thought, 'Yes, this is it, I'm going to die now.'

Dad came to my rescue. He wrestled her to the floor and managed to pull her hands away from my neck. He shouted to me, 'GET OUT NOW!'

I ran out of the sitting room so fast, the door slammed shut and I stayed outside the door to catch my breath before going out onto the balcony to join my cousins.

My cousins asked me what was going on and I told them all that had happened. They were scared, very scared. I could see the look on their faces. While I was still speaking to them, my mother appeared at the doorway, looked at me and told me, 'I am no longer your mother. Your father is your mother and

54

father from now on. If you need anything, go to him. Do not come to me.'

I was speechless. Mum walked past me and went down the stairs onto the street. I was so unhappy that my life was the way it was. My cousins just stared at me in pity.

Dad came to the door and said he was taking my cousins home and asked me to come along. We followed him downstairs to the car. Dad drove all the way to my cousins' home in silence. When we got to the front of their house, we all said goodbye to each other. Dad said I should stay in the car while he took them indoors. He was soon back in the car and we drove back home again in silence.

My cousins never came to our house again. I believe it was because of what they had seen my mother do. For the rest of the summer Mum refused to cook or care for me and left this to my dad. Dad did try his best. Sometimes I went hungry. She rarely spoke to me, but made sure I did my chores – with definite repercussions if I did not. I did not feel secure in my own home during that summer. I would pray in the toilet before my mother came home from work, that I would not be beaten by her that day. I wondered many times whether God heard, especially when I would still get beaten for one reason or the other. During that time I did nothing right in my mother's view.

Broken teeth

I can remember that in September 1975, when I started secondary school, my father also gained admission to the University of Sunderland, to study Pharmacy. My father had worked so hard that year to pass his examinations. His desire was to become a pharmacist. I was very happy for him; however, his admission to the university would mean that he would have to live on the campus away from home. That was a scary thought. I was going to be living alone with my mother, not knowing what my fate would be. In what state would my father find me when he came home on holidays? Would I still be alive?

I felt much safer when I was away from home; unfortunately at this point in time I was going to attend a new school. A secondary school, a gigantic school where I did not know anybody. Unlike other children who could talk to their parents, I could not. The anxiety, the trauma, of starting a new school had to be kept to myself, in my mind: there was no one to ask and no one to encourage me. Thankfully, I went to school and I enjoyed it.

At school I saw many children wearing nice straight blue skirts, white blouses and blue jumpers, not the old pleated skirts that I had used in my primary school, which my mother said that I still had to wear. My parents had bought the proper school uniform, but Mum was apparently keeping it until 'someday'. I knew where it was, however, so one day I wore it to school. She was not aware of this as she left home at 5.30 a.m. When I returned from school, happy that I could show off my school uniform to my friends, I put the uniform back exactly where I got it from, neatly folded. Little children with little minds do not think about the fact that the shirt would have a dirty neckline showing that it had been used, even though it was used only once.

I cannot remember what Mum was looking for that day, but she came across my white blouse that I had neatly put away. She pulled it out and brought it to my attention. I was scared. I did not know what to do. Should I tell the truth?

I did not tell the truth. I lied. I was beaten that day. I was literally flogged with wire. I thought that would be the end, until my mother lifted me up and threw me on the floor again. I landed on my face with two front teeth broken. There was blood all over the floor. I could feel my lips swelling and bleeding. I was crying. My mother did not say a word.

There was silence for a few minutes. Then Mum said I should go and clean my mouth with water. While I was rinsing my mouth, I looked into the mirror and saw my badly swollen lips and my two front teeth which were now damaged and cracked. I thought I looked like Dracula, I looked ugly.

I was given some food to eat that evening, but could not eat properly. My teeth had cut into my lips and had made them swollen and painful. I went to bed that night crying out to a God I did not know. I knew I had lied, but did I deserve this?

I was so embarrassed the next day, going to school with broken teeth. I could no longer smile with my friends. Even now, I still find it difficult to smile in public. I lied to them at school, saying that I had fallen down and broken my teeth. I stopped brushing my teeth due to the pain it caused.

My peers made fun of me at school, calling me names, and this made me sad. I would go to the toilet and cry. I had no one to talk to and no one at school enquired. My father was away in Sunderland studying at the university and so was not aware of what had happened.

Dad came home for a weekend in October and saw my new look. He asked me what had happened, and I told him that I lied to my mother about wearing my school blouse. My father asked if she had taken me to the dentist. I said, 'No.' He asked why not, and I said that I did not know. He asked me if my mother had actually done anything about my teeth. I said that no, she had only asked me to rinse my mouth. Dad was angry and went to Mum and shouted at her. All through the evening they were arguing. The following day, Dad phoned the dental department at King's College Hospital. We were given an appointment for the following day.

The next day I had to get up very early as my appointment was for ten o'clock. My father made me a cereal that morning. We then set out for the hospital. Dad did not have a car at that time, so we took a bus. When we got to the dental department there was a long queue. Dad spoke to me about what I should tell the dentist if he asked me what had happened. He said I should tell him that I fell over while playing with my friends.

I was scared when my name was finally called. I went into a room where I was asked to sit down in a big comfortable chair. I stretched out my legs and made myself comfortable. Next to the chair was a little sink with a cup that you could use to rinse out your mouth as your teeth are being cleaned. After a brief examination, I was told by the dentist that I would need to have an X-ray taken so that he could see the extent of the damage to my teeth. After taking the X-ray, the dentist told my father and I that I would need to have impressions of my teeth made and that they would need to be fitted on another visit. The dentist looked at the appointment log and gave us a date and time for the next appointment.

My dad told the dentist that he would not be around to bring me to the dentist then, as he would be back in Sunderland. He asked if there were any earlier appointments, but the dentist said it would take two weeks to make the impressions for my teeth and that was the reason for the long wait. Dad agreed to the appointment, but left the hospital that day with a dilemma. He was not sure whether my mum would take me to the dentist in his absence or not. I knew that she would not.

We walked out of the hospital to the bus stop. Dad tried to explain the directions from our house to the hospital by bus. Basically, he was saying to me that I would be coming to the hospital on my own. When we arrived home, I said hello to Mum and went into my room. My dad explained what had happened and asked if Mum would take me to the hospital. Mum answered, 'No.' I hated her for it, even though she only confirmed my expectations.

Dad went back to his university in Sunderland and on the day of the appointment I had to find my way back to the dental department of King's College Hospital by myself. I was frightened, but I knew that if I did not go I would remain ugly all the days of my life. I was desperate, but determined. Dad left me the return bus fare to King's College Hospital. I had never been alone on the buses before. At eleven years old, I just had to get on with it.

I tried to follow the directions my father gave me before he left. I had to take two buses. My mother saw me leave the house and could not care less. I managed not to get lost, and finally arrived at the hospital. When I got to the dentist, I was very anxious about what was going to happen. The dentist tried to put my heart at rest and explained that he would remove part of the broken teeth and set the impressions in place using a kind of cement. Then he would clean the teeth and polish them. I nodded my head and he got down to work.

He did a very good job. For the first time in a long time I could look in the mirror – but I could not smile. These were not my teeth. They were false teeth, even if they looked very real. However, I had to accept the fact that my teeth would never grow back again and the best I could do was to make use of the impressions I had been given.

I thought the teeth would last for ever. In fact, they fell out within five years. I have had dental treatment since then, but not once have I been able to tell the dentist the truth. How could I?

10

Home Alone Tragedy

There was an incident during the autumn half term of 1975 that changed my life altogether. This incident occurred two weeks after my my father had returned back to the university. My brother's childminder decided she was going on a long weekend, since it was school half term week. She was to be away from Friday to Monday. She gave my parents a week's notice. My parents thought it was a good idea if I went to school as normal on the Friday and the Monday and my younger sister, who was just seven years old, should stay at home alone babysitting our little brother, who was two and a half years old.

On the Friday, therefore, my sister and my brother stayed at home alone. My mother had left instructions as to what they should eat. They were meant to eat cereal for breakfast and have sandwiches for lunch. My sister, however, had plans of her own. She had made up her mind that she was going to make eggs, toast and hot tea. I was scared for both of them: what if someone came and took them away in our absence?

When I got back from school that day, I asked my sister what she had been up to. She told me about the

61

breakfast she had made that morning and all the TV programmes she had watched with our brother. I told her how risky it was for her to try cooking with no one else around, and I said I would have to tell our parents. When I mentioned it to Mum, though, she only told my sister off and warned her that she should do as she was told – that is, stick to the instructions she was given. If only she knew that a tragedy was about to happen! What a risk it was to leave a seven-year-old to babysit a toddler under three, home alone. My sister, unfortunately, had become very confident in her ability to fix a hot breakfast without training or supervision.

On the Monday, then, my sister and our brother were home alone again. At best it was a very risky arrangement, not to say downright dangerous. I went to school and our parents went to work. My sister repeated what she had done on the Friday. Her determination to be adventurous, in spite of warnings, was about to turn into a serious misadventure. It could all have been avoided if an adult had been at home with her and my brother, who was becoming quite a smart and active toddler at the time.

Shock news

I was picked up from school by two unknown men, who said to me that something bad had happened at home. I was afraid, not knowing what to think. I was then informed that my sister had suffered a fire accident at home and that she had been rushed to

Guy's and St Thomas' Hospital. I became more afraid and speechless. I was taken to the police station, where I was informed that my little brother had been taken into care. He had been taken to a children's home. The police officers saw how petrified I was and tried to put my mind at ease. They began to ask me a few questions. I was asked to confirm that my name was Ola Odetunde. The men also asked for my age and home address. I answered all their questions. I was given some tea and biscuits, then was asked to sit and wait in the waiting room for the social worker dealing with my case. The social worker was to take me to the children's care home where I would be staying until the case had been investigated.

The home where I was taken was for children between the ages of eight and 16. I was introduced to the care manager and shown where I would be sleeping. I saw a lot of other children, younger and older. There were children from various ethnicities. I arrived just in time for the evening meal, which I ate with the other children in the refectory. The home supervisor came to me and explained the rules of the home. She also gave me some information about my sister which she had obtained from the police. She told me that my sister had been severely burnt and would need to undergo a major operation in St Thomas' Hospital. I asked for details of what had happened. The supervisor took me to her office. She told me to sit down and gave me a summary of what had happened to my sister from an eye-witness's report.

That day my sister was wearing a yellow cardigan over a dress. The cardigan was not buttoned up. She was in the kitchen cooking, frying eggs, boiling the kettle and making toast under the grill. She was not tall enough, however, and had to make use of a nearby stool in the kitchen. The cardigan was loose and stretched over the gas cooker and caught fire.

At this point in her explanation, the supervisor saw that I had bowed down my head and was crying. She put her arms round me, telling me that everything would be all right. She asked if I wanted to hear the rest of the story. I said that I did.

She continued by saying that as the flames began to engulf my sister, my brother shouted that his sister was on fire, a nearby neighbour was able to break open the door, run inside with a fire blanket and wrap it around my sister, other neighbours came to the rescue and called the emergency services – and that was how she was rushed to the hospital.

By this time I was really sobbing. Why did my life have to be so hard? The supervisor held me close. I asked her if I could go and see my sister, but she explained that my sister was still not conscious, she was in shock. She told me that after my sister had gone through the operation I could go in and see her. The supervisor took me to my room for the night and whispered, 'Everything is going to be all right.' I changed into the nightgown I had been given. By that time, all the other children seemed to have gone to sleep. The lady said goodnight and I answered her, still crying. There I was, lying in a strange bed, not knowing what the future held for me. I was afraid, sad and anxious for my siblings. I cried myself to sleep.

Contrast in care

The next morning, I got up, brushed my teeth, had a shower and put on my school uniform. The night before, I had made a new friend during dinner. She was the only one who came over to me and asked how I was. She wanted to make sure that I was all right. She cared. We went to breakfast together that morning, and I was taken to school by a social worker who was to assist me in getting to know the route back to the home after school.

I was treated very well at that home. I really felt cared for and loved. Deep in my heart I was hoping that I would be able to live in the home for ever, away from the emotional, physical and psychological abuse and trauma I had received at the hands of my parents.

I was at the home for six weeks. During the fourth week my parents were allowed to come and see me. They were provided with a private room to speak with me. My dad asked how I was. Mum wanted to know what I had been asked at the police station and what my responses were. Dad told me that I had been brainwashed by the police. He also warned me not to say anything else to anybody, if I was asked any further questions about what went on in our home. Dad told me about my little brother, and said he was OK. Fortunately, he was not injured in the incident. Dad told me that they had been to see him and that he was being well taken care of.

I had not seen my parents for four weeks and to be honest, I did not miss them. At least I had not been beaten for four weeks. I did not really enjoy the visit from my parents that day; they seemed to be more interested in themselves. I got the impression that they came really to intimidate me into not revealing the facts about our family to the police. My mother brought out a notebook and said, 'You must take notes and keep a journal of all the events, questions anybody asks you and your answers as well.' The visit with my parents lasted about an hour. Then they got up and walked to the door. The care manager spoke with them briefly and they were seen out of the home.

The following weekend one of the home supervisors came to see me in the television room to inform me that I could go to the hospital to see my sister. She had been through a six-hour operation and it was successful. I cried again, this time for joy that my sister was going to live. I went to bed that night but could not sleep – so many questions crossed my mind. What would my sister look like now? What would her face look like? What would her skin look like? Would I be able to look at her? Would I be able to recognize her?

Visiting my sister

The next day I got up very early, dressed and had something to eat. The care manager had told me how I could get to St Thomas' Hospital. She said I would require two buses. She also told me that my sister was on the Children's Ward. She said, 'When you get to the hospital, ask the receptionist for directions to the Children's Ward.' On the way to the hospital, I was worried again, thinking about the state in which I would see my sister. When the bus stopped in front of the hospital, I saw how huge the building looked from the outside and I asked myself, 'Won't I get lost in this place?' I saw the main entrance sign and walked towards it. I went through the double doors, still apprehensive. On my right was a reception desk. I went over to the desk, scarcely taking notice of anything else around. I requested directions to the Children's Ward.

The lady at the reception desk was very kind and said I would need to take the lift. She told me which floor the Children's Ward was on. I headed towards the lifts. There were quite a lot of people trying to get in. My small size enabled me to squeeze myself into the lift. The lift arrived on the Children's Ward floor, I got out and started looking for signage to the ward. I followed the directions and got closer to the ward entrance. It looked beautiful – the best place for a child to recover from illness. I even thought to myself, 'I wouldn't mind staying here!' I saw a nurse taking care of the children, assisting some to move around.

I went over to the nurse, introduced myself and asked about my sister. I was told that she was in bed and likely to be asleep. The nurse said she had been in a very critical condition, but had successfully come through the six-hour operation. My heart was racing as the nurse guided me over to my sister's bed. I was getting scared again. As we approached, tears began to fill my eyes. She was asleep, peacefully asleep. She was covered in bandages around her legs, her chest and abdomen and her arm, and her thumb was in a glass container almost double the size. I asked the nurse, 'Why are there so many bandages?' The nurse gently told me that all the skin on her chest had been burnt off. She had to undergo a skin-graft operation. That meant that skin had to be taken from her legs to cover her chest and abdomen. The nurse told me that it was very bad. She had been brought into the hospital with no skin on her chest at all. I imagined the pain she must have had to bear, and shed some more tears.

I did not know what to do or say. I wiped my tears and thanked the nurse for explaining everything to me. I wanted to hold my sister, but I did not know how. We did not hug or kiss in my home, and I did not know whether I could touch my sister as she lay in the hospital bed. After a while of watching my sister asleep, I left the hospital without her knowing that I came. I felt grieved and very unhappy. I took the lift down to the ground floor and walked out of the hospital entrance to the bus stop, still in shock and feeling for my sister both the pain she had gone through and the pain she must still be in. I got home and told the supervisor how my day had been. She made me a cup of tea and took me to the television room. I sat on a chair and soon fell asleep.

I went back to the hospital to see my sister again a few days later. This time I met my mother there. She did not know that I had been a couple of days before then. She told me the story again – that my sister had undergone a six-hour operation which also involved skin-grafting because the burns were so severe. She had bad burns on her chest, stomach and sides, and also on her thumb. It dawned on me that my sister could have died. I then asked my mum what had really happened in the house that Monday morning. Mum gave me the same description of events that the home supervisor had given me. When I heard all the details again, I cried once more.

I did not stay too long as my sister was still fast asleep. I told my mother that I was leaving, and she said goodbye. It was amazing that in public Mum acted like an angel, fooling a lot of people into believing that she was a very nice person. How could she get away with it so easily?

Court

I did not realize then that what had happened to my sister was going to end up in a court of law. One day soon after that, however, I was informed by the manager at the home that the police investigating the case had indeed referred it to the courts. My parents were being taken to court on a number of charges, including child neglect. If they were found guilty, they would lose us for good and would not be able to gain access to see us.

After about five weeks at the home, I was told we had to go to court. I went with my social worker. We sat a distance away from my parents and I made sure I did not look their way. I did not wish to meet their gaze. The trial had started and the solicitors were doing what they do best. I think I got a bit concerned when they wanted to pass around the pictures of my sister's injuries and burns. I could not look at the pictures that were shown as evidence that day. I was too scared. I was worried that if I looked at them I would not sleep, and the memory would stay in my mind for ever. My parents were informed of the reasons why they were in court. They were told that they had broken the law by leaving my younger sister and brother at home alone. This was a criminal offence, because both children were under age. The older of the two was only seven and the younger one was not even three years old. I do not really remember the rest of the detail, but the case was adjourned. I left the court with my social worker, who escorted me back to the home.

After the hearing that day I decided to go and see my sister in hospital. I saw that now she was walking around and looking much better. The nurses loved her and cared so much for her. She did not look completely recovered from her trauma, but I was grateful to God that at least she was alive. I could not put my feelings into words or actions: I just stood there and looked at my sister. I was just so happy she was well. I did not know how to hug or kiss her; I just kept my hands to myself. Finally I summoned up courage and asked her how she was. She told me she was OK. I asked if she knew when she would leave the hospital, but she said she did not know and did not really want to leave. She wanted to stay in the hospital for good.

I knew why: she knew what abuse we had gone through with our parents. We both understood that she was in a much safer place – in the hospital. But who could we tell? Nobody would believe us anyway. Nobody asked about or investigated our past. Social Services seemed to have forgotten their previous calls at our home on my behalf. The lawyers did not dig that deep.

A travesty of justice

A couple of weeks later, we were back in court to hear the verdict. I cannot remember what was said. All I do know was that my parents were pronounced not guilty. What could be further from the truth? I did not understand what technicality must have swung in their favour.

Finally our parents were allowed to take us back home. I cannot explain my feelings that afternoon: they were more or less mixed, as I remembered how we had been treated while living with them. I was happy to be reunited with my siblings, with whom I had bonded and whom I had grown to love, but I was sad and scared of what might lie ahead for us at the hands of our parents. Uncertain that this was the best outcome for the family, I was shocked and confused at such a blatant miscarriage of justice in court. I felt let down by everyone who could have rescued us there and then.

I was escorted back to the home to pack my belongings. I was meant to be happy. I cried in court, but people thought it was for joy. It was not. It was because I knew that life was going to be exactly as it was before we ended up in care. When my parents came to pick me up, I could see that my brother had already been collected. I was sad to leave the home, because I knew deep down in my heart that I had been cared for and loved there much better than I had ever been since leaving my foster parents in Hastings.

I put my belongings in the car and off we went. Dad drove us home in silence. As we approached Dorset Road, my heart was gripped with fear. What was it going to be like? We got out of the car and climbed up the stairs to the third floor of Lulworth House with our luggage. My heart was pounding. When I got into the house I noticed that there had been a few changes. The kitchen had been changed around. The gas cooker had been replaced by an electric cooker. The only person not in the house was my sister, who was to be discharged soon.

My sister eventually came out of hospital eight weeks after the incident, and was brought home by my dad. I did most of the caring for my sister, trying to soften the grafting on her stomach using Nivea cream. My parents said this had been recommended by the doctors.

11

The Final Betrayal

Mum tried to be nice to us at first. It lasted for just about a month, after which she returned to her normal way of beating us mercilessly, despite the fact that my sister had been through such an ordeal. My sister needed tender loving care, and I was scared to touch her. My mother was always blaming my sister for what had happened to her. She argued that it was a result of her disobedience. My sister and I believed this for many years – until we realized that it was a way of blaming us for the situation, rather than our parents taking the blame for their negligence.

After my sister's accident and the disappointment of not getting into a grammar school, my parents decided it was best for my sister and me to be sent to Nigeria. Why did I have to go to Nigeria, when I was already doing well at school? I believed it was not my fault that I didn't get into a grammar school. Maybe my parents could explain why. Why did I say this?

I actually passed my entrance examination to a secondary school; the problem occurred when my parents got angry and started to shout at the school authority during the parents' interview. During the

1970s even when children were successful at the secondary school entrance examinations, it was part of the interview process to interview the child's parents too.

As for my sister's fire accident, it was not my sister's fault either. But because the social services were likely to keep an eye on my mum and dad with regard to child neglect, our parents felt it best to send us to Nigeria. Why did we have to suffer the consequences of our parents' actions? It was not fair, but we had to do as we were told. We had no choice in the matter.

Preparations began to fly my sister and me to Nigeria. We were both led to believe that we were going to there on a holiday, but this was a mere pretence. My parents got us all Nigerian passports, including our younger brother. Why couldn't we be given British passports? Maybe they thought we would never return to the UK again; even though we were all born here. It was also decided that we needed to have family photographs taken before the journey to Nigeria. So off we went to the photographer's studio. We spent almost three hours there while various photographs were taken with us wearing different types of clothing. The photographer must have told me over twenty times to smile, as I would never show my teeth. I did not see myself as pretty since my mother broke my two front teeth. When I did smile, it was usually not genuine. You can only really smile when you are happy within yourself. It is what is within a person that comes out in their emotions and behaviour. It is a pity that I never got a copy of any of the photographs taken since 1976 till this day. I wonder what the main reason was for taking the photographs that day.

During that same period, around late July, my parents decided that my sister's birthday and mine should be celebrated. My sister's birthday was in June and mine in July. My parents thought it was a good way to appease the gods regarding my sister's fire accident, just in case they had done something wrong. I don't know whether any sacrifices were made but we had a party which in Yoruba language is called *Saraa* to celebrate. Many people were invited; some I did not know and some I did. None of my friends or my sister's were invited. We were not even given the opportunity to invite anybody. Was this really a birthday party for my sister and me? I was twelve years old and my sister was eight. I had to be involved in the cooking of the dishes to be used; I had to cut and cook the fresh, whole chickens and prepare the black-eye beans for the bean pouches – *moinmoin* – that needed to be made.

Our clothes were purchased without our knowledge; all we knew was that they were going to be sewn by a tailor. We were dressed up in native Nigerian attire – we first wore red and golden lace robes, and a few hours later we were asked to change into royal blue and golden lace robes. A few hours later we were asked to change into children's evening dresses. Just imagine, we had to change our clothes three times just to celebrate this combined event. Pictures were taken at every occasion possible. I did not enjoy it one bit. It was as if we were doing all this for formality. I was asked to smile for the photographs, which was so hard. The party lasted late into the night. And yes, my sister and I had to do most of the cleaning up.

The day was fast approaching for our departure to Nigeria. Two days after the celebration we had to go to the hospital for our vaccinations against cholera, yellow fever, TB and malaria. The doctor also gave us some Nivaquine tablets to take. They were bitter and horrible. I found it difficult to swallow tablets so had to chew them instead. It got so bad that whenever my mother gave me the tablets I would throw them away.

Three weeks prior to leaving the UK my dad asked me a question I never expected to hear in my life, 'Would you like to go and see your foster parents in Hastings and maybe spend a week with them?'

I was delighted, it was the best news I had heard for the last seven years. 'Yes, Daddy, I would like to go.'

My father made a telephone call to my foster parents to let them know I would be coming. I packed a few of my clothes ready for the journey. I thought my father was going to drive me to Hastings, so I was shocked to hear that I was to be dropped at Loughborough Junction British Rail station in South West London and my foster parents were to pick me up on arrival at Hastings.

Home again!

The day finally arrived, and my father dropped me at the station a few minutes before my train arrived. I said goodbye to him and boarded the train.

Travelling alone was a scary experience. I stared out of the window and soon fell asleep. I did not know exactly when we arrived in Hastings but I was awoken by the sound of a whistle.

I soon saw a couple beckoning to me, 'Ola, Ola we are here.' I looked in their direction but I didn't recognise my foster parents any more – it was seven years since I had seen them last. I went over to them and said 'Hello', smiling briefly. 'What is the matter? Are you not happy to see us?' they said. I didn't understand what the matter was – what exactly were they expecting of me? Then my foster mum said, 'What has happened to you? You used to be all bubbly, outgoing and smiley. Why are you so quiet?'

I could not answer, I did not know how to answer, I did not know what to say. All I did know was that my whole life had been changed, I didn't know how to play or smile. I didn't know how to hug or kiss. My being had been battered by physical abuse I had sustained at the hands of my parents.

How could I begin to tell my foster parents about my ordeal? Would it have made matters better or worse? As a child I believed it would have made it worse, especially because my mother had warned me that I should never tell anybody about the abuse as if I did I would never forget what she would do to me. How was I to tell them about all the traumatic experiences? Would my foster parents tell my parents off? How could I tell them that my mother had thrown me on the floor and broken my two front teeth, how could I? I was too scared. I had been turned into a lonesome, insecure and rather quiet girl. I sat at the back of the car with my foster mum.

She spoke to me quietly, while my foster dad drove us home.

I was to spend a week. If only I could have stayed forever. I was determined to make the very best of the time. The week had been planned to include going to the fields to play with my foster siblings and pick berries for the fruit pie, and a trip to the seaside with the whole family followed by a visit to the funfair. These were the sort of things that I had got used to when I stayed with my foster parents when I was much younger.

My foster mother asked me what I thought of the plan and whether there was anywhere else I wanted to go. When I answered 'That's fine' my foster mum was a bit surprised that I did not make any additional suggestions. I was prepared to go ahead with everything she said. I was used to staying home on my own on so many occasions, without going out to play or being taken out on trips with my biological parents. Did it matter whether I went anywhere at all?

I went to the fields with my foster siblings and just walked and walked. I did not say much, what exactly was I to say? My answers were either 'Yes' or 'No', what else was there to say? Looking back on that time now, I can only imagine what was going through the minds of my foster family – they must have felt that I was acting strangely or that I didn't want to be there with them. I did try to be warm and open to conversation but it just didn't work. We picked a lot of berries that day and we walked together all the way home. My foster siblings were very caring and looked after me. When we arrived home, mum was waiting for the berries as she had started making the pastry for the pie. 'Ola I hope you enjoyed yourself?' she asked. I replied, 'Yes Mum, I did. We have brought back quite a few berries for the pie.' With this I gave Mum the berries and she sat down and looked at me, she looked at me quite strangely but I did not understand what was going through her mind. If only she had been more forceful with her questions she might have been able to rescue me. That afternoon I stayed with her in the kitchen and helped with the baking. I really did love her but I didn't know how to tell her so. I was so afraid to tell her, but why?

That evening we had a light supper, followed by pie and custard. After the meal we sat down to watch the TV. There was no particular programme I was interested in, I just watched whatever was on. I was soon dozing off when my foster mum noticed and asked, 'Ola, do you want to go to bed now, would you like some Ovaltine too?' Mum then made the hot drink and I went to my bedroom. I changed into my nightdress, had my drink, brushed my teeth and went to bed. I did not fall asleep immediately but started to think how nice it would be to stay there forever. If only ...

I woke the next day to a knock on my door. 'Ola wake up, we're going to the seaside today.' I had almost forgotten the plan for the week. I jumped out of bed, had a shower and brushed my teeth. I got myself dressed and then went downstairs for my breakfast. I did not have a swimsuit or anything for the seaside but my foster mum had said she would get one for me the day before. She had actually packed this along with a towel in the hamper we were going to take to the beach. My foster mum had been up early making the sandwiches and cakes we were to take for a picnic.

At the beach I changed into my swimsuit. My foster parents and siblings noticed the scars on my body and asked me, 'Ola, what is that on your back and arms?' I said nothing, remembering what my biological mother had warned me about telling anybody about my ordeal of abuse. I then said very slowly, 'I fell down while at school and scraped my side on the playground floor.' I knew I had lied and I was not so sure that my foster parents believed my story, but I was hoping the conversation would end there.

I didn't want to go into the sea so I stayed on the beach. My behaviour must have seemed strange but I didn't know this. I just didn't feel like really doing anything. I could sit in one place for a long time, even if it meant doing nothing.

We spent about three hours at the beach as it was such a beautiful sunny day. I sat on the beach chair and stared into the sea. If only this experience could last forever, so peaceful. I began thinking about my journey to Nigeria in a few days' time and really hoped it could be changed. I didn't mind if my parents disowned me and gave me the opportunity to say with my foster parents forever.

We all got into the car after packing up and throwing away all rubbish. As we drove home my foster parents were talking quietly to each other while I sat in the back pondering about what was to happen when I returned to my biological parents the next day. When we got home, we unloaded everything back into the house. We were all nicely exhausted and easily fell asleep that night.

The next morning I was the last to wake up, but was well rested in my body. My foster mum sat by me and told me she had something to tell me. I was afraid – had I done something wrong? Was I in trouble? My foster mum then said, 'Ola, you seem scared. It's alright, I just want to ask you a question.' With this she put her arm around me and said, 'Ola, your dad and I have been thinking about you, we would really like you to stay with us if you would like to. I have already looked for a secondary school for you. Remember I told you that I am a matron at a girls' school in Hastings? I will pay your fees and take care of you. Ola, what do you think?' Deep down in my heart I was so happy, but didn't know how to express myself so just replied, 'That would be nice but I would have to ask my parents first. You could ask them too.' I knew that my parents would not agree. I also knew I was not even bold enough to ask my parents anything, let alone asking about staying with another family. However, my foster parents did agree to ask my parents about it. The answer was no.

It was finally the day to return to London. My foster mum gave me a few snacks and a drink for the journey. My foster father and mother drove me to the station where they hugged and kissed me. I felt so loved and tears filled my eyes. My foster parents whispered in my ear, 'Ola, we love you.' I really didn't want to leave but I had to.

From home to home

I got into the train and sat myself down. As the train left the station I could see my foster parents waving at me, I waved back trying so hard to keep back the tears. The train journey went smoothly and as the train approached Loughborough Junction I could see my father waiting on the platform. I was not very happy to be back with my biological parents; I was so sad that I had to leave my foster parents. I walked alongside my father, carrying my luggage. He asked whether I had enjoyed my holiday and I told him that I had. That was all that was said as we walked to the car park. My father unlocked the car door and I got inside. We drove home in silence. When we arrived home, I said hello to my mother and she responded with 'Hello'. That was all. I knew that I was in trouble once more.

I had something to eat that night and I was told by my father that the packing had to be finalised tomorrow as the flight was in two days' time. I unpacked my case and put my clothes into the suitcase I was to travel to Nigeria with. My foster mother had already done my laundry for me. This was a very special feeling as my parents had not ever done my washing for me; I had to learn to wash my clothes by hand in the bathroom sink. I had to wash my school uniform and my sister's every Friday night and get them ironed.

During this time my sister was still recovering from her burns and was going for regular checkups. I was involved in putting Nivea cream on her chest and stomach region every evening. My sister's consultant had informed my parents that this should soften her skin in preparation for further plastic surgery.

Journey to Nigeria 17 August 1976

The day finally arrived for us to head to Heathrow airport where our plane was destined for Nigeria. That morning I was full of apprehension – what on earth am I getting into, should I have told my foster parents to keep me for good myself? Did they have the legal support to do so? I became very restless. The plan was that my father would stay in the UK and my mother would take my brother, my sister and me to Nigeria. My mother and brother would return home but my sister and I would be left in Nigeria to attend school there. My sister and I didn't actually understand that going to Nigeria meant we were going to be forced into a rollercoaster experience of being moved from home to home. Many of the places we were to go, we knew neither the friends or relations of our parents but we had to stay with them anyway.

All this flooded my mind as we were on our way to the airport in my father's car. When we arrived we quickly moved to the checking-in area. Our luggage was checked and we all walked together to the departure lounge, where, for the first time in my life, my father kissed me. After the kiss he said goodbye. I just looked at him and I saw the tears in his eyes but I couldn't understand why he was crying. I kept that picture in my mind for a very long time.

Within a few minutes there was an announcement

the the flight to Lagos, Nigeria was ready for boarding. With this my mother, brother, sister and I boarded the aircraft. My mum sat with my brother and I sat next to my sister. I was so afraid of aeroplanes and crashes, but couldn't tell anyone, not even my parents. I was not sure we would get to Nigeria without our plane having some problems. I decided to pray to the God. I didn't really know, but believed he would answer my prayer. I prayed seven times, 'God, please don't let us have an accident, let us get to Nigeria safely.'

I did not sleep throughout the six-hour journey. I was apprehensive of what Nigeria would be like; I was not given any advice or information. My mother did not speak to us until we touched down at Muritala Mohammed Airport, Lagos. We successfully got through immigration within minutes. By the time we got out of the airport relatives were waiting to take us to a place called home. We all said hello to our aunty and uncle and then got into the car, beginning our journey to an unknown destination. The person driving the car was driving so fast, I was scared. I questioned why he was doing this and overtaking other cars with no regard as to whether we had an accident and got injured. Nobody said a word, not even my mother.

I decided to take my mind off of what was going on in the car, so I looked out of the window and saw flames of fire in front of some houses. What was going on, what kind of a country was this where people cook in front of their houses using wood and large pots? I was shocked, amazed, troubled and apprehensive. Was I going to enjoy my stay here or not? I had to discover the answers to all those questions by way of experience. It was a very hard learning experience – there is an adage that says 'experience is the best teacher'. My life in Nigeria without my parents for three whole years was an experience on its own. I cover this period of my life in my next book.

By the time my sister returned to England some years later she was in her twenties, and learnt that she could only have the required treatment for her burns if she paid for it privately. The NHS staff informed her that after her eighteenth birthday she was no longer covered under the NHS for that particular form of treatment. By then, it was considered cosmetic surgery.

12

Reflections

What hardship there was in those early years of my life! God gives life, and he can take it away.

I had no friends during my childhood days. Who could I talk to about my experiences? The social workers were lied to and never returned. I did not know how to contact them. I really wanted to run away from the place I was meant to call 'home', but where could I go? I was very scared, so very scared. I was not aware of organizations like the NSPCC, and ChildLine was not in existence at the time. I was emotionally, mentally and physically wounded. I could not speak to anyone or disclose anything. I could not trust anyone. Most of all, I could not even trust my parents.

I am alive today because God wanted me to live to tell my story, my true story. For many years I cried over my wounds and scars, I had lost all self-esteem and confidence in myself, I was totally crushed inside. I could not smile because of my broken teeth. I could not style my hair in a particular way because of the bald patches left by my injuries. My memories and scars still bring tears to my eyes, but healing is a continuous process. I do not know how long it will take, but I do believe that one day my healing will be complete.

There was a struggle going on inside me for many years, a struggle of revenge and hatred towards my mother and father – but one day I took a decision to forgive them for all they had done to me. I cried before God that day, I sobbed for quite a long time. Why *should* I forgive them? The Lord took me back to the Bible, to the description of Jesus being crucified on the cross. Jesus said, 'Father, forgive them, for they do not know what they are doing' (Luke 23:34). I cried all the more from the pain of my memories. Eventually I asked God to give me the strength to forgive and also to heal me from within. You can imagine why this was a very hard thing for me to do. I can now talk about some of the memories without feeling emotional, but it is still difficult at times.

Did I feel loved?

There were some instances in my early years when I did feel loved. I certainly felt loved when I was in foster care in Hastings, and when I had to stay in the children's home for a short period of time following my sister's fire accident. I also felt loved when I went to hospital with my head injury and the nurse cared for me so well and kindly. Yet these instances were few and far between – and the people who showed me love were not my parents. That may seem shocking, but it is the truth.

Since I forgave my parents, I have been able to

love them as human beings. I do not hold any of the abuse against them. I have done quite a few things for them. If I had not forgiven them, I would never have done those things. I have had to show love to them, even though I did not experience love *from* them. I have been able to shop for food for them and I have taken our children to visit them, so as to facilitate a relationship. Our children need to know who their grandparents are.

But what is love? The dictionary definition is all about showing a strong affection to someone or something. Love is reciprocal: if someone expresses love to you, you will automatically express it back. That is what human beings believe, but it is not always the case. Sometimes you still need to show love to people even when they hate you. The love I am talking about is the unconditional love of God. It is not based on what people do. It is about showing love regardless of what they do. God showed all mankind love by sending his only begotten Son to die for us. We can receive his love and believe that he showed his love by his death on the cross. He rose again and is alive in all those who receive him into their hearts. Everyone can be loved and can love if they choose to.

Final comments

Please do not leave your children home alone unless they have reached the appropriate age under law. In the UK that age is 13, and then only if the child is deemed responsible by his or her parents.

Please show your children that you love them. Of course there are times when discipline should be given, but give careful consideration to what is discipline and what is abuse. There is perhaps a slim line between the two. If you have a conscience you will know the difference. Do not hurt your child. The child may never talk about it, and may never forgive you.

Build a relationship with your children, so that in your old age you will have them around you to show you love. They will also learn how to have fruitful relationships, not least with their own children. Develop a relationship with your child, get to know your child, so that you can rest assured of what your child can or cannot do. Find time to spend with your children, have times to play and laugh together. Never think that work is more important than family. Find time for the family: money is not everything.

Do not teach your children to lie. Instead teach them to be children of integrity, always telling the truth and facing up to their actions, especially in a culture where people tend to blame somebody else, or the government, for everything. Words, good and bad, are indelible once stored in the mind (especially in a child's mind) and, once spoken, often cannot be forgotten.

Try not to say negative, horrible or spiteful words to your children. Learn to tell your children that you love them, hug them and kiss them. I have had to teach myself to do this with my own children. I do not remember my parents ever kissing me.

I would like to ask you a question. If you went through this kind of ordeal, or worse, can you find space in your heart to forgive? Please try to forgive and move on.

Finally, this is my life and my story. It was hard, it was traumatic, but in the end I found myself able to forgive and move on in a positive way. I hope parents, carers and guardians of children will learn and be encouraged by this. I also hope that both young and adult victims of abuse will find healing and the strength to forgive. It is my sincere hope that no other child will be made to suffer the treatment that was meted out to me. I felt I had no one to turn to at the time, but help is available now. If you are a young person still going through any form of abuse, please get help: phone ChildLine, or your local Social Services.

USEFUL CONTACT DETAILS

Stop it Now! UK & Ireland
Central Administrator: Anna Lord
Bordesley Hall
The Holloway
Alvechurch
Birmingham
B48 7QA
Tel: 01527 598184
Email: office@stopitnow.org.uk
For confidential emails: help@stopitnow.org.uk

Stop it Now! Scotland
National Manager: Martin Henry
Tel: 0131 556 3535
Email: scotland@stopitnow.org.uk
For confidential emails: help@stopitnow.org.uk

Stop it Now! Wales
National Manager: Rebecca Wasinski
Tel: 07989378220
Email: wales@stopitnow.org.uk
For confidential emails: help@stopitnow.org.uk

Stop it Now! England
National Manager: Liz Maslen
Tel: 01527 406915
Email: lmaslen@stopitnow.org.uk
For confidential emails: help@stopitnow.org.uk

Stop it Now! London
Regional Manager: Helen Veitch
Tel: 0207 428 1080
Email: hveitch@stopitnow.org.uk
For confidential emails: help@stopitnow.org.uk

Stop it Now! Black Country & Birmingham
Project Co-ordinator: Martine McFadden
Tel: 01384 561 775
Email: blackcountry@stopitnow.org.uk
For confidential emails: help@stopitnow.org.uk

Stop it Now! Northern Ireland
Project Contact: Anna Lord
Tel: 01527 598184
Email: office@stopitnow.org.uk
For confidential emails: help@stopitnow.org.uk

AFRUCA (Africans Unite Against Child Abuse)
Tel: 0844 660 8607
Fax: 0844 660 8661
Samaritans
Tel: 08457 909090

National Society for the Prevention of Cruelty to Children (NSPCC) in England, Wales and Northern Ireland
Freephone 0800 800 500

Irish Society for the Prevention of Cruelty to Children (ISPCC)
Tel: 01 6767 960 (from within Ireland)

Children First
Tel: 0131 446 2300

ChildLine
Tel: 0800 11 11

Kidscape
Tel: 020 7730 3300

Parentline Plus
Tel: 0808 800 2222